WORD by WORD

BASIC
PICTURE DICTIONARY

Steven J. Molinsky · Bill Bliss

PRENTICE HALL REGENTS, Upper Saddle River, NJ 07458

Library of Congress Cataloging-in-Publication Data

Molinsky, Steven J.
　　Word by word picture dictionary / Steven J. Molinsky, Bill Bliss.
　　　　p.　cm.
　　Abridged version of Word by word picture dictionary.
　　Includes index.
　　ISBN 0-13-278565-X (paper) : 8.00
　　1. Picture dictionaries, English　2. English language—Textbooks for foreign speakers.
I. Bliss, Bill.　II. Molinsky, Steven J.　Word by word picture dictionary.　III. Title.
PE1629.M582　1995　　　423'.1—dc20　　　95-717 CIP

Publisher: *Tina Carver*
Director of Production & Manufacturing: *David Riccardi*
Electronic Production/Design Manager: *Dominick Mosco*
Production editor, interior design and electronic composition: *Steven K. Jorgensen*
Cover design: *Paul Belfanti*
Design Coordinator: *Merle Krumper*
Production Coordinator: *Ray Keating*

Illustrated by RICHARD E. HILL

© 1995 by Prentice Hall Regents
Prentice-Hall, Inc.
Simon & Schuster / A Viacom Company
Upper Saddle River, New Jersey　074582

Printed in the United States of America
10　9　8　7　6　5

ISBN 0-13-278565-X

Prentice-Hall International (UK) Limited, *London*
Prentice-Hall of Australia Pty. Limited, *Sydney*
Prentice-Hall Canada Inc., *Toronto*
Prentice-Hall Hispanoamericana, S. A., *Mexico*
Prentice-Hall of India Private Limited, *New Delhi*
Prentice-Hall of Japan, Inc., *Tokyo*
Simon & Schuster Asia Pte. Ltd., *Singapore*
Editora Prentice-Hall do Brasil, Ltda., *Rio de Janeiro*

The *Word by Word Basic Picture Dictionary* presents over 1500 vocabulary words through lively full-color illustrations. This innovative Picture Dictionary offers students at the low-beginning and literacy levels of English the essential vocabulary they need for everyday language and survival needs. This text is an abridged version of the "full" *Word by Word Picture Dictionary*.

Word by Word Basic organizes the vocabulary into 67 thematic units, providing a careful sequence of lessons that range from the immediate world of the student to the world at large. Early units on the family, the home, and daily activities lead to lessons on the community, school, workplace, shopping, and other topics. *Word by Word Basic* provides coverage of important lifeskill competencies and the vocabulary of school subjects and extracurricular activities. Since each unit is self-contained, *Word by Word Basic* can be used either sequentially or in any desired order.

For users' convenience, the units of *Word by Word Basic* are listed in two ways: sequentially in the Table of Contents, and alphabetically in the Thematic Index. These resources, combined with the Glossary in the appendix, allow students and teachers to easily locate all words and topics in the Picture Dictionary.

The *Word by Word Basic Picture Dictionary* is the centerpiece of the complete *Word by Word Basic Vocabulary Development Program*, which offers a wide selection of print and media support materials for instruction at the low-beginning and literacy levels. Ancillary materials include Beginning and Literacy level Workbooks, a Teacher's Resource Book, a complete Audio Program, Wall Charts, Color Transparencies, Vocabulary Game Cards, a Song Album and accompanying Songbook, and a Testing Program. Bilingual editions of the Basic Picture Dictionary are also available.

Teaching Strategies

Word by Word Basic presents vocabulary words in context. Model conversations depict situations in which people use the words in meaningful communication. These models become the basis for students to engage in dynamic, interactive conversational practice. In addition, writing and discussion questions in each unit encourage students to relate the vocabulary and themes to their own lives as they share experiences, thoughts, opinions, and information about themselves, their cultures, and their countries. In this way, students get to know each other "word by word."

In using *Word by Word Basic*, we encourage you to develop approaches and strategies that are compatible with your own teaching style and the needs and abilities of your students. You may find it helpful to incorporate some of the following techniques for presenting and practicing the vocabulary in each unit.

1. *Previewing the Vocabulary:* Activate students' prior knowledge of the vocabulary either by brainstorming with students the words in the unit they already know and writing them on the board, or by having students look at the Wall Chart, the transparency, or the illustration in *Word by Word Basic* and identify the words they are familiar with.

2. *Presenting the Vocabulary:* Point to the picture of each word, say the word, and have the class repeat it chorally and individually. Check students' understanding and pronunciation of the vocabulary.

3. *Vocabulary Practice:* Have students practice the vocabulary as a class, in pairs, or in small groups. Say or write a word, and have students point to the item or tell the number. Or, point to an item or give the number, and have students say the word.

4. *Model Conversation Practice:* Some units have model conversations that use the first word in the vocabulary list. Other models are in the form of *skeletal dialogs,* in which vocabulary words can be inserted. (In many skeletal dialogs, bracketed numbers indicate which words can be used to practice the conversation. If no bracketed numbers appear, all the words on the page can be used.)

The following steps are recommended for Model Conversation Practice:

a. Preview: Students look at the model illustration and discuss who they think the speakers are and where the conversation takes place.

b. The teacher presents the model and checks students' understanding of the situation and the vocabulary.

c. Students repeat each line of the conversation chorally or individually.

d. Students practice the model in pairs.

e. A pair of students presents a new conversation based on the model, but using a different word from the vocabulary list.

f. In pairs, students practice several new conversations based on the model, using different vocabulary words.

g. Pairs present their conversations to the class.

5. *Writing and Spelling Practice:* Have students practice spelling the words as a class, in pairs, or in small groups. Say or spell a word, and have students write it and then point to the picture of the item or tell the number. Or, point to a picture of an item or give the number, and have students write the word.

6. *Themes for Discussion, Composition, Journals, and Portfolios:* Each unit of *Word by Word Basic* provides one or more questions for discussion and composition. (These can be found in a green-shaded area at the bottom of the page.) Have students respond to the questions as a class, in pairs, or in small groups. Or, have students write their responses at home, share their written work with other students, and discuss as a class, in pairs, or in small groups.

Students may enjoy keeping a journal of their written work. If time permits, you may want to write a response in each student's journal, sharing your own opinions and experiences as well as reacting to what the student has written. If you are keeping portfolios of students' work, these compositions serve as excellent examples of students' progress in learning English.

7. *Communication Activities:* The *Word by Word Basic* Teacher's Resource Book provides a wealth of games, tasks, brainstorming, discussion, movement, drawing, miming, role-playing, and other activities designed to take advantage of students' different learning styles and particular abilities and strengths. For each unit, choose one or more of these activities to reinforce students' vocabulary learning in a way that is stimulating, creative, and enjoyable.

Word by Word Basic aims to offer students a communicative, meaningful, and lively way of practicing English vocabulary. In conveying to you the substance of our program, we hope that we have also conveyed the spirit: that learning vocabulary can be genuinely interactive . . . relevant to our students' lives . . . responsive to students' differing strengths and learning styles . . . and fun!

Steven J. Molinsky
Bill Bliss

WORD by WORD

BASIC

PICTURE DICTIONARY

1. name
2. first name
3. middle name
4. last name
5. address
6. street number
7. street
8. apartment number
9. city
10. state
11. zip code
12. area code
13. telephone number/ phone number
14. social security number

A. What's your **name**?
B. *Nancy Ann Peterson.*

Tell about yourself:
  My name is ....
  My address is ....
  My telephone number is ....
Now interview a friend.

1. wife
2. husband

parents
3. mother
4. father

children
5. daughter
6. son
7. sister
8. brother
9. baby

grandparents
10. grandmother
11. grandfather

grandchildren
12. granddaughter
13. grandson

A. Who is she?
B. She's my **wife**.
A. What's her name?
B. Her name is *Betty*.

A. Who is he?
B. He's my **husband**.
A. What's his name?
B. His name is *Fred*.

Tell about your family.
Talk about photos of family members.

1. aunt
2. uncle
3. niece
4. nephew
5. cousin

6. mother-in-law
7. father-in-law
8. son-in-law
9. daughter-in-law
10. brother-in-law
11. sister-in-law

A. Who is she?
B. She's my **aunt**.
A. What's her name?
B. Her name is *Linda*.

A. Who is he?
B. He's my **uncle**.
A. What's his name?
B. His name is *Jack*.

Tell about your relatives:
What are their names?
Where do they live?
Draw your family tree and talk about it.

1. get up
2. take a shower
3. brush *my** teeth
4. floss *my** teeth
5. shave
6. get dressed
7. wash *my** face
8. put on makeup
9. brush *my** hair
10. comb *my** hair
11. make the bed

12. get undressed
13. take a bath
14. go to bed
15. sleep
16. make breakfast
17. make lunch
18. cook/make dinner
19. eat/have breakfast
20. eat/have lunch
21. eat/have dinner

* my, his, her, our, your, their

A. What do you do every day?
B. **I get up**, **I take a shower**, and **I brush my teeth**.

What do you do every day?
   Make a list.
Interview some friends and tell about their everyday activities.

1. clean the apartment/ clean the house
2. sweep the floor
3. dust
4. vacuum
5. wash the dishes
6. do the laundry
7. iron
8. feed the baby
9. feed the cat
10. walk the dog
11. watch TV
12. listen to the radio
13. listen to music
14. read
15. play
16. play basketball
17. play the guitar
18. practice the piano
19. study
20. exercise

A. Hi! What are you doing?
B. I'm **clean**ing **the apartment**.

What are you going to do tomorrow?
(Tomorrow I'm going to _____, _____, _____, ...)

1. teacher
2. teacher's aide
3. student
4. seat/chair
5. pen
6. pencil
7. eraser
8. desk
9. teacher's desk
10. book/textbook
11. notebook
12. notebook paper
13. graph paper
14. ruler
15. calculator
16. clock
17. flag
18. board
19. chalk
20. chalk tray
21. eraser
22. P.A. system/loudspeaker
23. bulletin board
24. thumbtack
25. map
26. pencil sharpener
27. globe
28. bookshelf
29. overhead projector
30. TV
31. (movie) screen
32. slide projector
33. computer
34. (movie) projector

A. Where's the **teacher**?
B. The **teacher** is *next to* the **board**.

A. Where's the **pen**?
B. The **pen** is *on* the **desk**.

Describe your classroom.
(There's a/an ....)

1. Stand up.
2. Go to the *board*.
3. Write *your name*.
4. Erase *your name*.
5. Sit down./Take your seat.

6. Open *your book*.
7. Read *page eight*.
8. Study *page eight*.
9. Close *your book*.
10. Put away *your book*.

11. Listen to *the question*.
12. Raise *your hand*.
13. Give *the answer*.
14. Work *in groups*.
15. Help *each other*.

Practice these classroom actions.

You're the teacher!
Give instructions to your students.

1. Do *your homework.*
2. Bring in *your homework.*
3. Go over *the answers.*
4. Correct *your mistakes.*
5. Hand in *your homework.*

6. Take out *a piece of paper.*
7. Pass out *the tests.*
8. Answer *the questions.*
9. Check *your answers.*
10. Collect *the tests.*

11. Lower *the shades.*
12. Turn off *the lights.*
13. Turn on *the projector.*
14. Watch *the movie.*
15. Take notes.

Practice these classroom actions.

You're the teacher!
Give instructions to your students.

1. apartment (building)
2. (single-family) house
3. duplex/two-family house
4. townhouse/townhome
5. condominium/condo
6. dormitory/dorm
7. mobile home/trailer
8. farmhouse
9. cabin
10. nursing home
11. shelter
12. houseboat

A. Where do you live?
B. I live in an **apartment building**.

Tell about people you know and the types of housing they live in.
Discuss:
    Who lives in dormitories?
    Who lives in nursing homes?
    Who lives in shelters?
    Why?

1. coffee table
2. rug
3. floor
4. armchair
5. end table
6. lamp
7. lampshade
8. window
9. drapes/curtains
10. sofa/couch
11. pillow
12. ceiling
13. wall
14. wall unit/entertainment unit
15. television
16. video cassette recorder/VCR
17. stereo system
18. speaker
19. loveseat
20. plant
21. painting
22. frame
23. mantel
24. fireplace
25. fireplace screen
26. picture/photograph
27. bookcase

A. Where are you?
B. I'm in the living room.
A. What are you doing?
B. I'm *dusting** the **coffee table**.

*dusting/cleaning

Tell about your living room.
(In my living room there's
............)

1. (dining room) table
2. (dining room) chair
3. china cabinet
4. china
5. chandelier
6. buffet
7. salad bowl
8. pitcher
9. serving bowl
10. serving platter
11. tablecloth

12. candlestick
13. candle
14. centerpiece
15. salt shaker
16. pepper shaker
17. butter dish
18. serving cart
19. teapot
20. coffee pot
21. creamer
22. sugar bowl

A. This **dining room table** is very nice.
B. Thank you. It was a gift from my *grandmother.**

*grandmother/grandfather/
aunt/uncle/...

Tell about your dining room. (In my dining room there's ....)

1. salad plate
2. bread-and-butter plate
3. dinner plate
4. soup bowl
5. water glass

6. wine glass
7. cup
8. saucer
9. napkin

silverware
10. salad fork
11. dinner fork
12. knife
13. teaspoon
14. soup spoon
15. butter knife

A. Excuse me. Where does the **salad plate** go?
B. It goes *to the left of* the **dinner plate**.

A. Excuse me. Where does the **soup spoon** go?
B. It goes *to the right of* the **teaspoon**.

A. Excuse me. Where does the **wine glass** go?
B. It goes *between* the **water glass** and the **cup and saucer**.

A. Excuse me. Where does the **cup** go?
B. It goes *on* the **saucer**.

Practice giving directions. Tell someone how to set a table. (Put the ....)

1. bed
2. headboard
3. pillow
4. pillowcase
5. sheet
6. blanket
7. electric blanket
8. bedspread
9. comforter/quilt
10. footboard
11. blinds

12. night table/nightstand
13. alarm clock
14. clock radio
15. chest (of drawers)
16. mirror
17. jewelry box
18. dresser/bureau
19. twin bed
20. mattress
21. box spring
22. double bed

23. queen-size bed
24. king-size bed
25. bunk bed
26. trundle bed
27. sofa bed/convertible sofa
28. day bed
29. cot
30. water bed
31. canopy bed
32. hospital bed

A. Ooh! Look at that big bug!!
B. Where?
A. It's on the **bed**!
B. I'LL get it.

Tell about your bedroom. (In my bedroom there's ....)

1. dishwasher
2. dishwasher detergent
3. dishwashing liquid
4. faucet
5. sink
6. (garbage) disposal
7. sponge
8. scouring pad
9. pot scrubber
10. dish rack
11. paper towel holder
12. dish towel
13. trash compactor
14. cabinet
15. microwave
16. counter
17. cutting board
18. canister
19. stove/range
20. oven
21. potholder
22. toaster
23. spice rack
24. can opener
25. cookbook
26. refrigerator
27. freezer
28. ice maker
29. ice tray
30. kitchen table
31. placemat
32. kitchen chair
33. garbage pail

A. I think we need a new **dishwasher**.
B. I think you're right.

Tell about your kitchen.
(In my kitchen there's
............)

1. teddy bear
2. intercom
3. chest (of drawers)
4. crib
5. mobile
6. night light
7. changing table/ dressing table
8. diaper pail
9. toy chest
10. doll
11. swing
12. playpen
13. stuffed animal
14. rattle
15. cradle
16. walker
17. car seat
18. stroller
19. baby carriage
20. food warmer
21. booster seat
22. baby seat
23. high chair
24. portable crib
25. baby carrier
26. potty

A. Thank you for the **teddy bear**. It's a very nice gift.
B. You're welcome.

Tell about your country: What things do people buy for a new baby? Does a new baby sleep in a separate room, as in the United States?

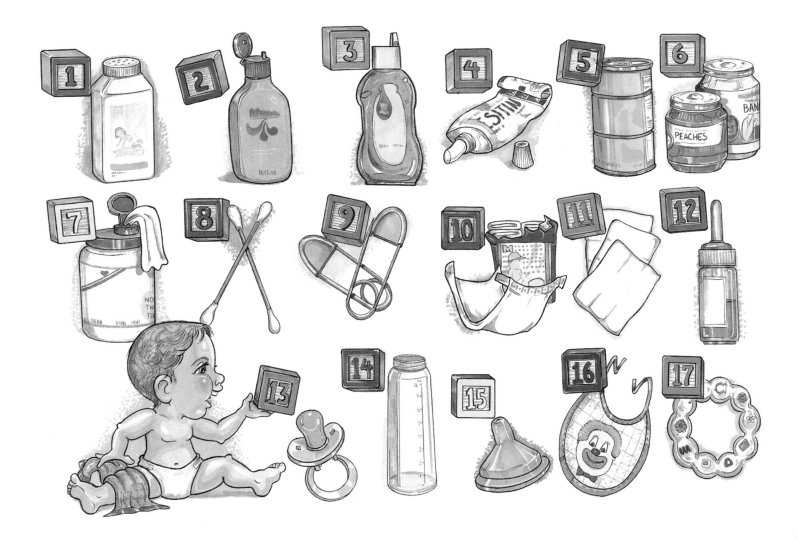

1. baby powder
2. baby lotion
3. baby shampoo
4. ointment
5. formula
6. baby food
7. (baby) wipes
8. cotton swabs
9. diaper pins

10. disposable diapers
11. cloth diapers
12. (liquid) vitamins
13. pacifier
14. bottle
15. nipple
16. bib
17. teething ring

[1–12]
A. Do we need anything
   from the store?
B. Yes. Please get some
   more **baby powder**.

[13–17]
A. Do we need anything
   from the store?
B. Yes. Please get another
   pacifier.

Tell about baby products in your country.

1. plunger
2. toilet
3. toilet seat
4. air freshener
5. toilet paper
6. toilet brush
7. towel rack
8. towel
9. hamper
10. scale
11. hair dryer
12. fan
13. mirror
14. medicine cabinet/
    medicine chest

15. sink
16. faucet
17. toothbrush
18. soap
19. soap dispenser
20. Water Pik
21. vanity
22. wastebasket
23. shower
24. shower curtain
25. bathtub/tub
26. drain
27. rubber mat
28. sponge
29. bath mat

A. Where's the **plunger**?
B. It's next to the **toilet**.

A. Where's the **mirror**?
B. It's over the **sink**.

A. Where's the **towel**?
B. It's on the **towel rack**.

Tell about your bathroom.
(In my bathroom there's
............)

1. toothbrush
2. comb
3. brush
4. razor
5. razor blades
6. electric razor/electric shaver
7. shower cap
8. nail clipper
9. scissors
10. tweezers
11. shampoo
12. conditioner
13. hairspray
14. powder
15. toothpaste
16. mouthwash
17. dental floss
18. shaving creme
19. after shave lotion
20. deodorant
21. perfume/cologne
22. nail polish
23. lipstick
24. shoe polish
25. makeup

[1–10] A. Excuse me. Where can I find **toothbrush**es?
B. They're in the next aisle.
A. Thank you.

[11–25] A. Excuse me. Where can I find **shampoo**?
B. It's in the next aisle.
A. Thank you.

You're going on a trip. Make a list of personal care products you need to take with you.

1. broom
2. dustpan
3. iron
4. ironing board
5. vacuum cleaner
6. hand vacuum
7. mop
8. washing machine/washer
9. dryer
10. paper towels

11. utility sink
12. sponge
13. trash can/garbage can
14. laundry basket
15. bucket/pail
16. scrub brush
17. recycling bin
18. clothesline
19. clothespins

A. Excuse me. Do you sell **brooms**?
B. Yes. They're at the back of the store.
A. Thanks.

Who does the cleaning and laundry in your home? What things does that person use?

1. lamppost
2. mailbox
3. front porch
4. front door
5. doorbell
6. window
7. shutter
8. roof
9. TV antenna
10. chimney

11. garage
12. garage door
13. driveway
14. deck
15. back door
16. satellite dish
17. patio
18. lawnmower
19. barbecue/grill
20. tool shed

A. When are you going to repair the **lamppost**?
B. I'm going to repair it tomorrow.

Do you like to repair things?
What things can you repair yourself?
What things can't you repair?
Who repairs them?

1. lobby
2. intercom
3. buzzer
4. mailbox
5. elevator
6. smoke detector
7. peephole
8. door chain
9. lock
10. air conditioner

11. fire alarm
12. garbage chute
13. laundry room
14. superintendent
15. storage room
16. parking garage
17. parking lot
18. balcony
19. swimming pool
20. whirlpool

A. Is there a **lobby**?
B. Yes, there is. Do you want to see the apartment?
A. Yes, please.

Tell about the differences between living in a house and in an apartment building.

1. carpenter
2. handyman
3. painter
4. chimney sweep
5. appliance repair person
6. TV repair person
7. locksmith
8. gardener
9. electrician
10. plumber
11. exterminator

12. gas bill
13. electric bill
14. telephone bill
15. water bill
16. oil bill/heating bill
17. cable TV bill
18. pest control bill
19. rent
20. parking fee
21. mortgage payment

A. Did you pay the **carpenter**?
B. Yes. I wrote a check yesterday.

Tell about utilities, services, and repairs you pay for. How much do you pay?

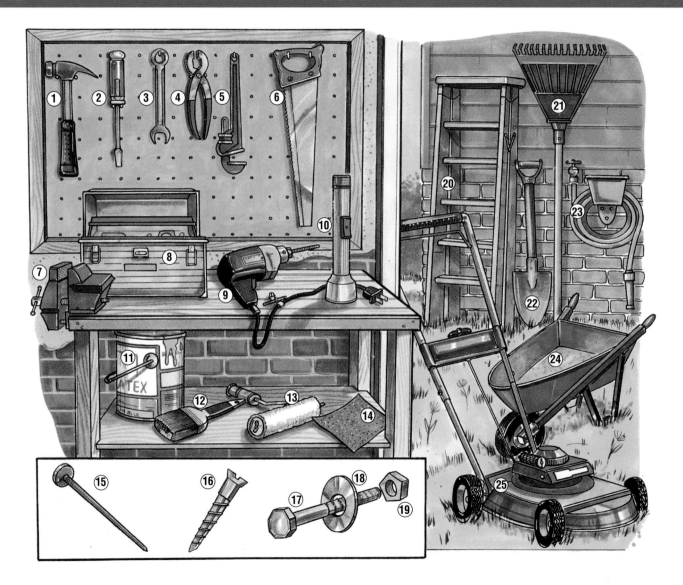

1. hammer
2. screwdriver
3. wrench
4. pliers
5. monkey wrench
6. saw
7. vise
8. toolbox
9. electric drill
10. flashlight
11. paint
12. paintbrush
13. paint roller

14. sandpaper
15. nail
16. screw
17. bolt
18. washer
19. nut
20. step ladder
21. rake
22. shovel
23. hose
24. wheelbarrow
25. lawnmower

A. Can I borrow your **hammer***?
B. Sure.
A. Thanks.

*With 11 and 14, use: Can I borrow some _____?
With 15–19, use: Can I borrow some _____s?

Do you like to work with tools?
What tools do you have in your home?

1 one	11 eleven	21 twenty-one	101 one hundred (and) one
2 two	12 twelve	22 twenty-two	102 one hundred (and) two
3 three	13 thirteen	30 thirty	1,000 one thousand
4 four	14 fourteen	40 forty	10,000 ten thousand
5 five	15 fifteen	50 fifty	100,000 one hundred thousand
6 six	16 sixteen	60 sixty	1,000,000 one million
7 seven	17 seventeen	70 seventy	
8 eight	18 eighteen	80 eighty	
9 nine	19 nineteen	90 ninety	
10 ten	20 twenty	100 one hundred	

A. How old are you?

B. I'm _____ years old.

A. How many people are there in your family?

B. _____.

1st	first	11th	eleventh	21st	twenty-first	101st	one hundred (and) first
2nd	second	12th	twelfth	22nd	twenty-second	102nd	one hundred (and) second
3rd	third	13th	thirteenth	30th	thirtieth	1000th	one thousandth
4th	fourth	14th	fourteenth	40th	fortieth	10,000th	ten thousandth
5th	fifth	15th	fifteenth	50th	fiftieth	100,000th	one hundred thousandth
6th	sixth	16th	sixteenth	60th	sixtieth	1,000,000th	one millionth
7th	seventh	17th	seventeenth	70th	seventieth		
8th	eighth	18th	eighteenth	80th	eightieth		
9th	ninth	19th	nineteenth	90th	ninetieth		
10th	tenth	20th	twentieth	100th	one hundredth		

A. What floor do you live on?
B. I live on the _____ floor.

A. Is this the first time you've seen this movie?
B. No. It's the _____ time.

Arithmetic

addition	subtraction	multiplication	division
2 **plus** 1 **equals*** 3.	8 **minus** 3 **equals*** 5.	4 **times** 2 **equals*** 8.	10 **divided by** 2 **equals*** 5.

*You can also say: **is**

Fractions

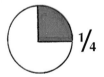    

one quarter/   one third   one half/   two thirds   three quarters/
one fourth   half   three fourths

Percents

twenty-five percent   fifty percent   seventy-five percent   one hundred percent

A. How much is two plus one?
B. Two plus one equals/is three.

Make conversations for the arithmetic problems at the top of page 50. Then make other conversations.

A. Is this on sale?
B. Yes. It's _____ off the regular price.

A. Is the gas tank almost empty?
B. It's about _____ full.

A. How did you do on the test?
B. I got _____ percent of the answers right.

A. What's the weather forecast?
B. There's a _____ percent chance of rain.

 **2:00**

two o'clock

 **2:15**

two fifteen
a quarter after *two*

 **2:30**

two thirty
half past *two*

 **2:45**

two forty-five
a quarter to *three*

 **2:05**

two oh five

 **2:20**

two twenty
twenty after *two*

 **2:40**

two forty
twenty to *three*

 **2:55**

two fifty-five
five to *three*

A. What time is it?
B. It's _____.

A. What time does the movie begin?
B. At _____.

two a.m.

two p.m.

noon
twelve noon

midnight
twelve midnight

A. When does the train leave?
B. At _____.

A. What time will we arrive?
B. At _____.

Tell about your daily schedule:
  What do you do?
  When?
  (I get up at _____.
  I ....)

Tell about time in different cultures or countries you are familiar with:
  Do people arrive on time for work? appointments? parties?
  Do trains and buses run on schedule?
  Do movies and sports events begin on time?
  Do workplaces use time clocks or timesheets?

1999	JANUARY	1999

SUN •	MON •	TUE •	WED •	THUR •	FRI •	SAT
					1	2
3	4	5	6	7	8	9
10	11	12	13	14	15	16
17	18	19	20	21	22	23
24/31	25	26	27	28	29	30

1. **year**

   nineteen ninety-nine

2. **month**

January	July
February	August
March	September
April	October
May	November
June	December

3. **day**

Sunday	Thursday
Monday	Friday
Tuesday	Saturday
Wednesday	

4. **date**

   January 2, 1999

   1/2/99

   January second, nineteen ninety-nine

A. What year is it?
B. It's _____.

A. What month is it?
B. It's _____.

A. What day is it?
B. It's _____.

A. What's today's date?
B. Today is _____.

When did you begin to study English?
What days of the week do you study English?
  (I study English on _____.)

When is your birthday? (My birthday is on _____.)
What is your favorite month of the year? Why?

1. bakery
2. bank
3. barber shop
4. book store
5. bus station
6. cafeteria

7. child-care center/ day-care center
8. cleaners
9. clinic
10. coffee shop
11. convenience store

A. Where are you going?
B. I'm going to the **bakery**.

Which of these places are in your neighborhood? (In my neighborhood there's a ....)

1. department store
2. drug store/pharmacy
3. flower shop/florist
4. gas station/
   service station
5. grocery store

6. hair salon
7. hardware store
8. health club
9. hospital
10. hotel

A. Hi! How are you today?
B. Fine. Where are you going?
A. To the **department store**. How
   about you?
B. I'm going to the **drug store**.

Which of these places are in your neighborhood? (In my neighborhood there's a ....)

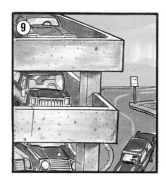

1. ice cream shop
2. laundromat
3. library
4. motel
5. movie theater
6. museum

7. music store
8. park
9. parking garage
10. parking lot
11. pet shop
12. pizza shop

A. Where's the **ice cream shop**?
B. It's right over there.

Which of these places are in your neighborhood? (In my neighborhood there's a/an ....)

1. post office
2. restaurant
3. school
4. shoe store
5. shopping mall
6. supermarket

7. theater
8. toy store
9. train station
10. video store
11. zoo

A. Is there a **post office** nearby?
B. Yes. There's a **post office** around the corner.

Which of these places are in your neighborhood? (In my neighborhood there's a ....)

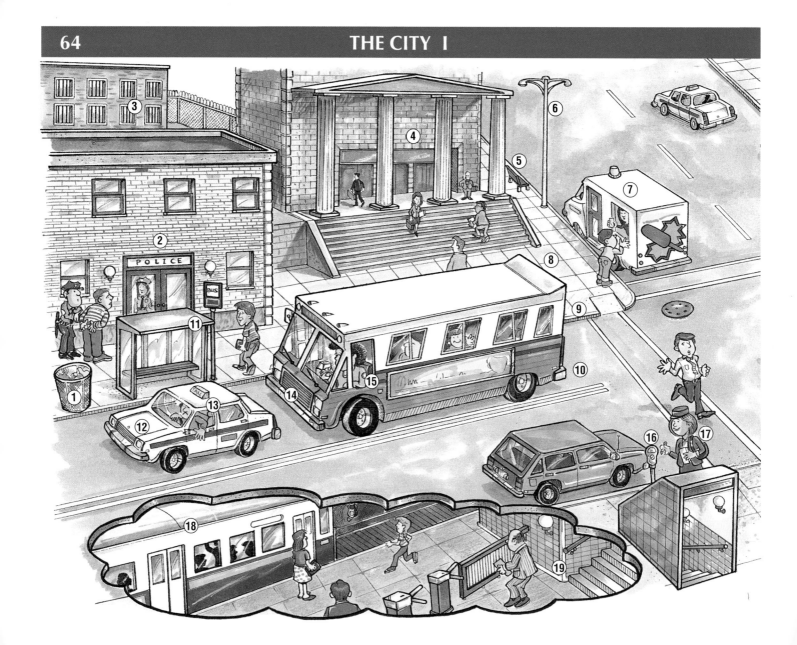

1. trash container
2. police station
3. jail
4. courthouse
5. bench
6. street light
7. ice cream truck
8. sidewalk
9. curb
10. street

11. bus stop
12. taxi/cab
13. taxi driver/cab driver
14. bus
15. bus driver
16. parking meter
17. meter maid
18. subway
19. subway station

A. Where's the _____?
B. On/In/Next to/Between/ Across from/In front of/ Behind/Under/Over the _____.

Which of these people, places, and things are in your neighborhood?

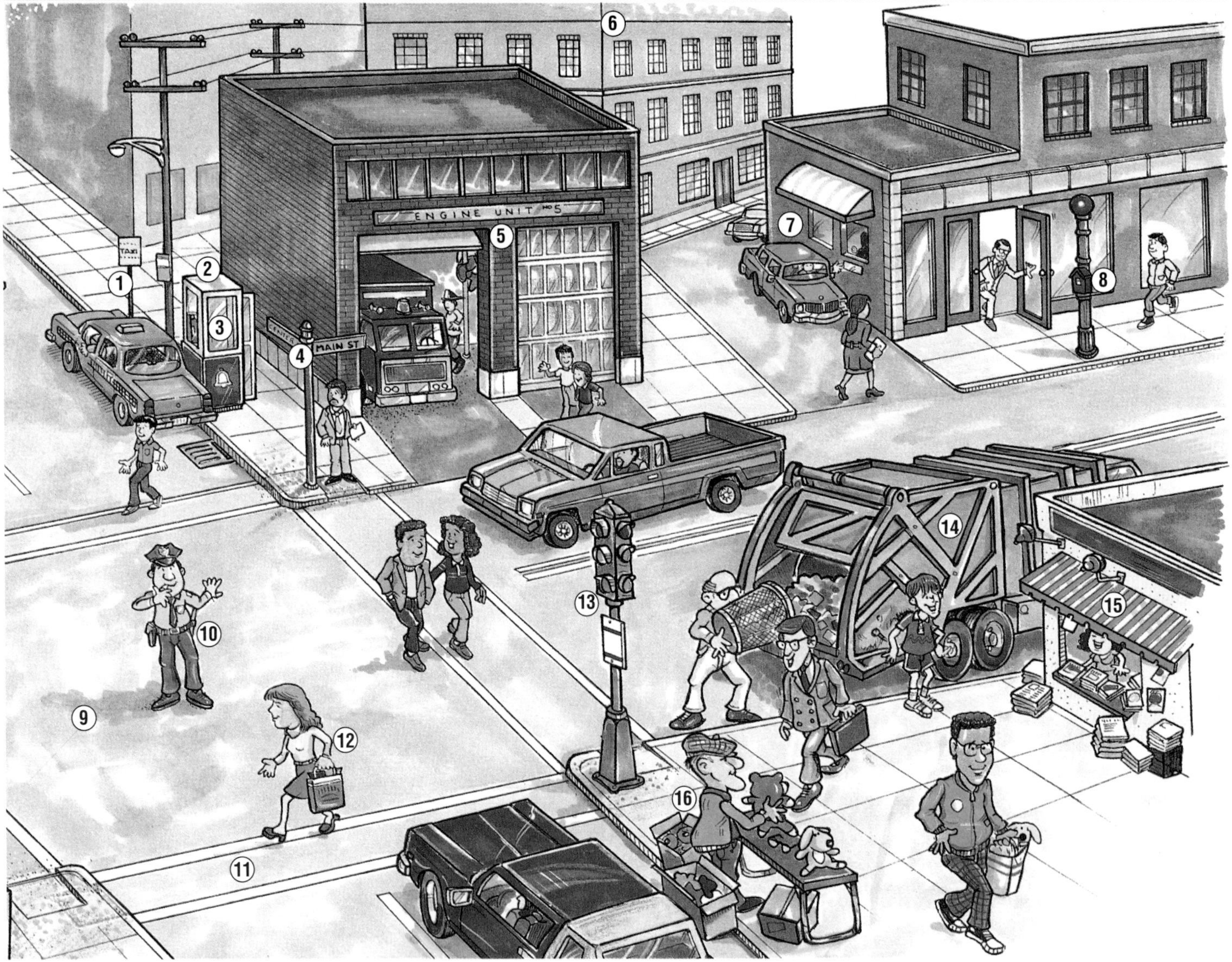
TAXI
ENGINE UNIT No 5
MAIN ST
1
2
3
4
5
6
7
8
9
10
11
12
13
14
15
16

1. taxi stand
2. phone booth
3. public telephone
4. street sign
5. fire station
6. office building
7. drive-through window
8. fire alarm box
9. intersection
10. police officer
11. crosswalk
12. pedestrian
13. traffic light
14. garbage truck
15. newsstand
16. street vendor

A. Where's the _____?
B. On/In/Next to/Between/
   Across from/In front of/
   Behind/Under/Over
   the _____.

Which of these people, places, and things are in your neighborhood?

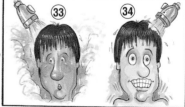

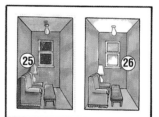

1–2	tall – short	**1–2**	Is your sister _____?
3–4	long – short	**3–4**	Is his hair _____?
5–6	large/big – small/little	**5–6**	Is their dog _____?
7–8	high – low	**7–8**	Is the bridge _____?
9–10	heavy/fat – thin/skinny	**9–10**	Is your friend _____?
11–12	heavy – light	**11–12**	Is the box _____?
13–14	loose – tight	**13–14**	Are the pants _____?
15–16	fast – slow	**15–16**	Is the train _____?
17–18	straight – crooked	**17–18**	Is the path _____?
19–20	straight – curly	**19–20**	Is his hair _____?
21–22	wide – narrow	**21–22**	Is that street _____?
23–24	thick – thin	**23–24**	Is the line _____?
25–26	dark – light	**25–26**	Is the room _____?
27–28	new – old	**27–28**	Is your car _____?
29–30	young – old	**29–30**	Is he _____?
31–32	good – bad	**31–32**	Are your neighbor's children _____?
33–34	hot – cold	**33–34**	Is the water _____?

[1–2]
A. Is your sister **tall**?
B. No. She's **short**.

Describe yourself.
Describe a person you know.
Describe one of your favorite places.

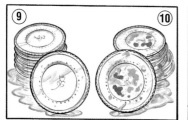

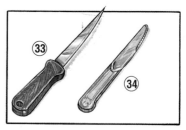

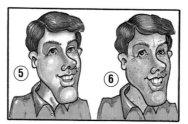

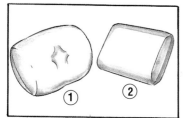

1–2	soft – hard
3–4	easy – difficult/hard
5–6	smooth – rough
7–8	neat – messy
9–10	clean – dirty
11–12	noisy/loud – quiet
13–14	married – single
15–16	rich/wealthy – poor
17–18	pretty/beautiful – ugly
19–20	handsome – ugly
21–22	wet – dry
23–24	open – closed
25–26	full – empty
27–28	expensive – cheap/inexpensive
29–30	fancy – plain
31–32	shiny – dull
33–34	sharp – dull

1–2	Is your pillow _____?
3–4	Is today's homework _____?
5–6	Is your skin _____?
7–8	Is your desk _____?
9–10	Are the dishes _____?
11–12	Is your neighbor _____?
13–14	Is your sister _____?
15–16	Is your uncle _____?
17–18	Is the witch _____?
19–20	Is the pirate _____?
21–22	Are the clothes _____?
23–24	Is the door _____?
25–26	Is the pitcher _____?
27–28	Is that restaurant _____?
29–30	Is the dress _____?
31–32	Is your kitchen floor _____?
33–34	Is the knife _____?

[1–2]
A. Is your pillow **soft**?
B. No. It's **hard**.

Describe yourself.
Describe a person
  you know.
Describe one of your
  favorite places.

1. tired
2. hot
3. cold
4. hungry
5. thirsty
6. full

7. sick
8. happy
9. sad/unhappy
10. disappointed
11. upset
12. annoyed

A. You look **tired**.
B. I am. I'm VERY **tired**.

What makes you happy?
What makes you sad?
When do you get annoyed?

1. frustrated
2. angry/mad
3. disgusted
4. surprised
5. nervous
6. worried

7. scared/afraid
8. bored
9. proud
10. embarrassed
11. jealous
12. confused

A. Are you **frustrated**?
B. Yes. I'm VERY **frustrated**.

What makes you angry? What makes you nervous? Do you ever feel embarrassed? When?

1. apple
2. peach
3. pear
4. banana
5. plum
6. apricot
7. nectarine
8. kiwi
9. papaya
10. mango
11. fig
12. coconut
13. avocado
14. cantaloupe
15. honeydew
16. pineapple

17. watermelon
18. grapefruit
19. lemon
20. lime
21. orange
22. tangerine
23. grapes
24. cherries
25. prunes
26. dates
27. raisins
28. blueberries
29. cranberries
30. raspberries
31. strawberries

[1–22]
A. This **apple** is delicious!
B. I'm glad you like it.

[23–31]
A. These **grapes** are delicious!
B. I'm glad you like them.

What fruits do you like?
Which of these fruits grow
    where you live?
What other fruits do you
    know?

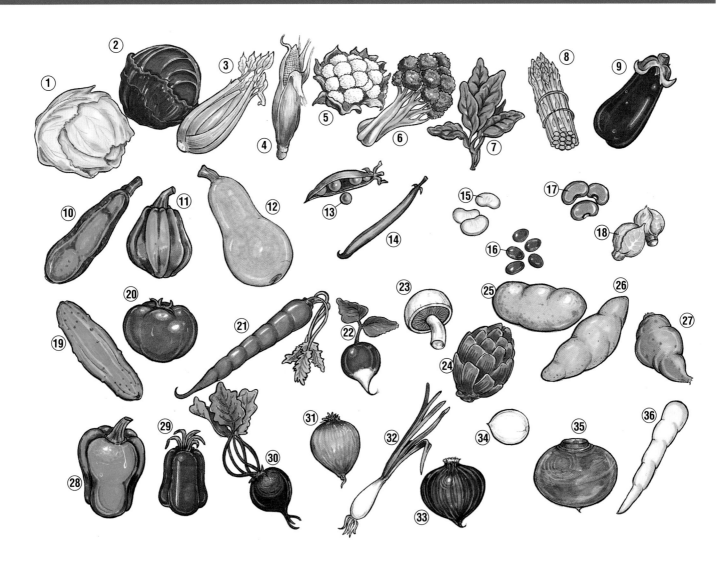

1. lettuce
2. cabbage
3. celery
4. corn
5. cauliflower
6. broccoli
7. spinach
8. asparagus
9. eggplant
10. zucchini
11. acorn squash
12. butternut squash
13. pea
14. string bean/green bean
15. lima bean
16. black bean
17. kidney bean
18. brussels sprout

19. cucumber
20. tomato
21. carrot
22. radish
23. mushroom
24. artichoke
25. potato
26. sweet potato
27. yam
28. green pepper
29. red pepper
30. beet
31. onion
32. scallion/green onion
33. red onion
34. pearl onion
35. turnip
36. parsnip

A. What do we need from the supermarket?
B. We need **lettuce*** and **pea**s.†

*1–12   †13–36

Which vegetables do you like?
Which of these vegetables grow where you live?
What other vegetables do you know?

1. milk
2. chocolate milk
3. cream
4. orange juice
5. cheese
6. butter

7. margarine
8. sour cream
9. cream cheese
10. cottage cheese
11. yogurt
12. eggs

A. What do we need from the supermarket?
B. We need **milk**.

Which of these foods do you like? Which foods are good for you?

1. mayonnaise
2. ketchup
3. mustard
4. salt
5. pepper
6. spices
7. oil
8. soy sauce
9. vinegar
10. flour
11. salad dressing
12. sugar
13. tissues
14. napkins
15. toilet paper
16. soap

17. paper towels
18. cereal
19. soup
20. cookies
21. juice
22. soda
23. crackers
24. cake
25. spaghetti
26. rice
27. noodles
28. coffee
29. tea
30. bread
31. rolls
32. ice cream

A. Do we need any **mayonnaise**?
B. Yes. Let's get some.

Which of these groceries do you buy?
What brands of these products do you buy?

1. ground beef
2. steak
3. lamb
4. pork
5. ham
6. bacon
7. chicken

8. turkey
9. fish
10. shrimp
11. clams
12. crabs
13. lobster

A. Do you want to get **ground beef**?
B. Sure. Good idea.

Which of these foods do you like? What foods are good for you?

1. aisle
2. shopping cart
3. shopper/customer
4. checkout counter
5. scale
6. cash register

7. cashier
8. plastic bag
9. paper bag
10. bagger/packer
11. express checkout line
12. shopping basket

A. This is a really big supermarket!
B. It is! Look at all the **aisle**s.

Describe the differences between U.S. supermarkets and food stores in your country.

1. bag
2. bar
3. bottle
4. box
5. bunch

6. can
7. carton
8. container
9. dozen

A. Please get a **bag** of *flour* at the supermarket.
B. A **bag** of *flour*? Okay.

What do you do with empty bottles and cans? Do you recycle them, reuse them, or throw them away?

1. jar
2. loaf-loaves
3. package
4. roll
5. pint

6. quart
7. half-gallon
8. gallon
9. liter
10. pound

A. Would you get a **jar** of *mayonnaise* at the supermarket?
B. A **jar** of *mayonnaise*? Sure.

Open your kitchen cabinets and refrigerator. Make a list of all the things you find.

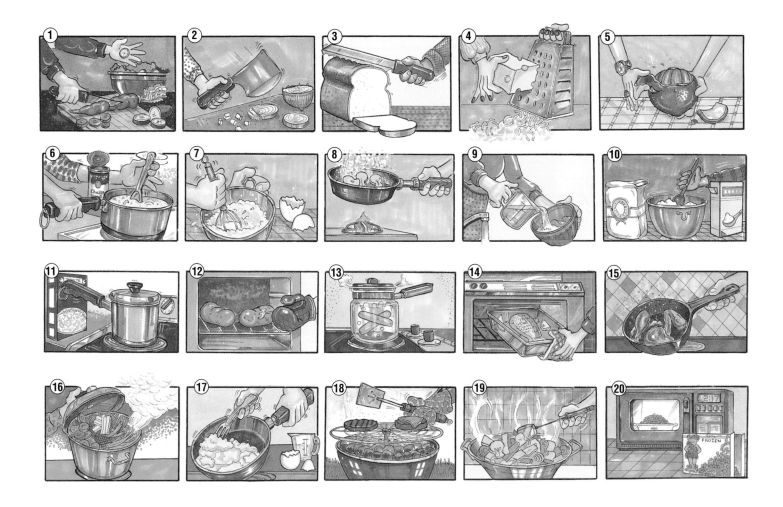

1. cut (up)
2. chop (up)
3. slice
4. grate
5. peel
6. stir
7. beat
8. saute
9. pour
10. mix

11. cook
12. bake
13. boil
14. broil
15. fry
16. steam
17. scramble
18. barbecue/grill
19. stir-fry
20. microwave

A. Can I help?
B. Yes. Please **cut up** the vegetables.

What's your favorite recipe?
Give the instructions.

1. donut
2. muffin
3. bagel
4. pastry
5. biscuit
6. hamburger
7. cheeseburger
8. hot dog
9. taco

10. pizza
11. sandwich
12. soda
13. lemonade
14. coffee
15. decaf coffee
16. tea
17. iced tea
18. milk

[1–11]
A. May I help you?
B. Yes. I'd like a **donut**, please.

[12–18]
A. What would you like to drink?
B. **Soda**.

Do you go to fast food restaurants? Which ones? What do you order?

1. booth
2. table
3. menu
4. high chair
5. booster seat

6. cook
7. dishwasher
8. waiter
9. waitress
10. busboy
11. cashier

[1–5]
A. Would you like a **booth**?
B. Yes, please.

[6–11]
A. Do you have any job openings?
B. Yes. We're looking for a **cook**.

Do you go to restaurants? Tell about a restaurant you know.

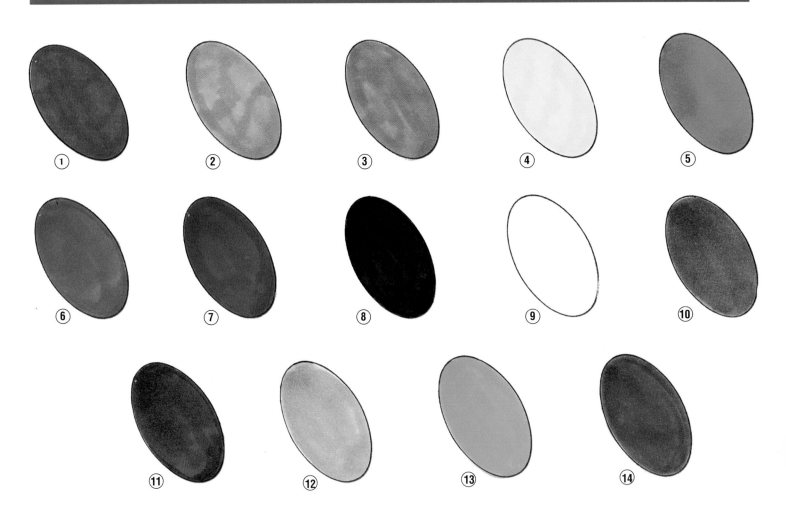

1. red
2. pink
3. orange
4. yellow
5. green
6. blue
7. purple

8. black
9. white
10. gray
11. brown
12. beige
13. light green
14. dark green

A. What's your favorite color?
B. **Red.**

What are the colors of flags you know?
What color makes you happy? What color makes you sad? Why?

1. shirt
2. blouse
3. pants/slacks
4. jeans
5. skirt
6. dress
7. shorts

8. sweater
9. uniform
10. sports jacket
11. suit
12. vest
13. tie

A. I think I'll wear my new **shirt** today.
B. Good idea!

What color clothes do you like to wear?
Do you ever wear jeans? When?

1. pajamas
2. nightgown
3. bathrobe
4. slippers
5. undershirt
6. underpants
7. boxer shorts
8. panties
9. briefs

10. bra
11. slip
12. stockings
13. pantyhose
14. socks
15. shoes
16. sneakers
17. boots
18. sandals

[1-14]
A. I can't find my new **pajamas**.
B. Look in the bureau/dresser/closet.

[15-18]
A. Those are very nice **shoes**.
B. Thanks.

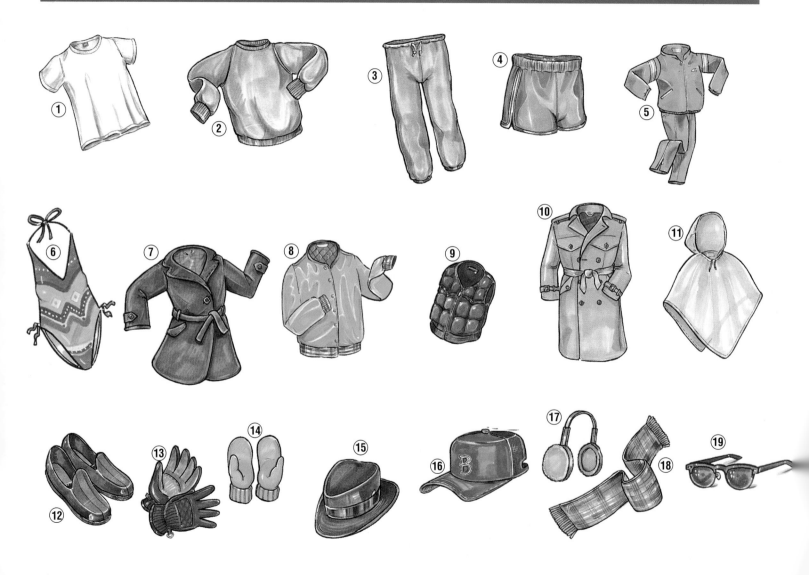

1. tee shirt
2. sweatshirt
3. sweat pants
4. running shorts
5. jogging suit
6. swimsuit
7. coat
8. jacket
9. down vest
10. raincoat

11. poncho
12. rubbers
13. gloves
14. mittens
15. hat
16. baseball cap
17. ear muffs
18. scarf
19. sunglasses

A. Excuse me. Is this/Are these your _____?
B. Yes. Thank you.

What do you wear when you exercise?
What do you wear outside when the weather is bad?

1. ring
2. wedding band
3. earrings
4. necklace
5. pin
6. watch
7. bracelet
8. cuff links
9. belt

10. key ring
11. wallet
12. change purse
13. pocketbook/purse
14. book bag
15. backpack
16. briefcase
17. umbrella

A. Oh, no! I think I lost my **ring**!
B. That's too bad!

Do you like to wear jewelry?
    What jewelry do you have?
In your country, what do men,
    women, and children use to
    carry their things?

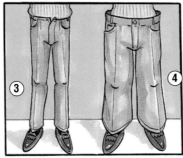
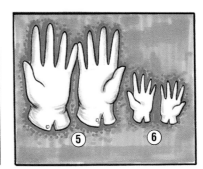

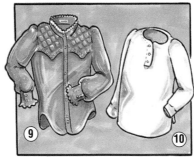
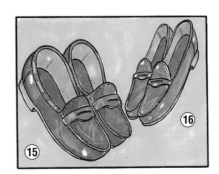

1–2	long – short	1–2	Are the sleeves too _____?	
3–4	tight – loose/baggy	3–4	Are the pants too _____?	
5–6	large/big – small	5–6	Are the gloves too _____?	
7–8	high – low	7–8	Are the heels too _____?	
9–10	fancy – plain	9–10	Is the blouse too _____?	
11–12	heavy – light	11–12	Is the coat too _____?	
13–14	dark – light	13–14	Is the color too _____?	
15–16	wide – narrow	15–16	Are the shoes too _____?	

[1-2]
A. Are the sleeves too **long**?
B. No. They're too **short**.

Describe your favorite clothing.

Name	Value		Written as:
1. penny	one cent	1¢	$ .01
2. nickel	five cents	5¢	$ .05
3. dime	ten cents	10¢	$ .10
4. quarter	twenty-five cents	25¢	$ .25
5. half dollar	fifty cents	50¢	$ .50
6. silver dollar	one dollar		$ 1.00

A. How much is a **penny** worth?
B. A penny is worth **one cent**.

A. Soda costs seventy-five cents.
   Do you have enough change?
B. Yes. I have a/two/three _____(s) and . . . .

Name	We sometimes say:	Value	Written as:
1. (one-)dollar bill	a one	one dollar	$ 1.00
2. five-dollar bill	a five	five dollars	$ 5.00
3. ten-dollar bill	a ten	ten dollars	$ 10.00
4. twenty-dollar bill	a twenty	twenty dollars	$ 20.00
5. fifty-dollar bill	a fifty	fifty dollars	$ 50.00
6. (one-)hundred dollar bill	a hundred	one hundred dollars	$100.00

A. Do you have any cash?
B. Yes. I have a **twenty-dollar bill**.

A. Can you change a **five-dollar bill**?
B. Yes. I've got *five* **one-dollar bill**s.

How much do you pay for a loaf of bread? a hamburger? a cup of coffee? a gallon of gas?
Name and describe the coins and currency in your country. What are they worth in U.S. dollars?

1. checkbook
2. bank book
3. credit card
4. ATM card
5. deposit slip
6. withdrawal slip
7. check

8. money order
9. vault
10. teller
11. security guard
12. ATM machine/ cash machine
13. bank officer

[1–4]
A. What are you looking for?
B. My _____.

[5–8]
A. What are you doing?
B. I'm filling out this _____.

[9–13]
A. How many _____s does the State Street Bank have?
B. . . . .

Do you have a bank account? What kind? Where?
Do you have a credit card? When do you use it?

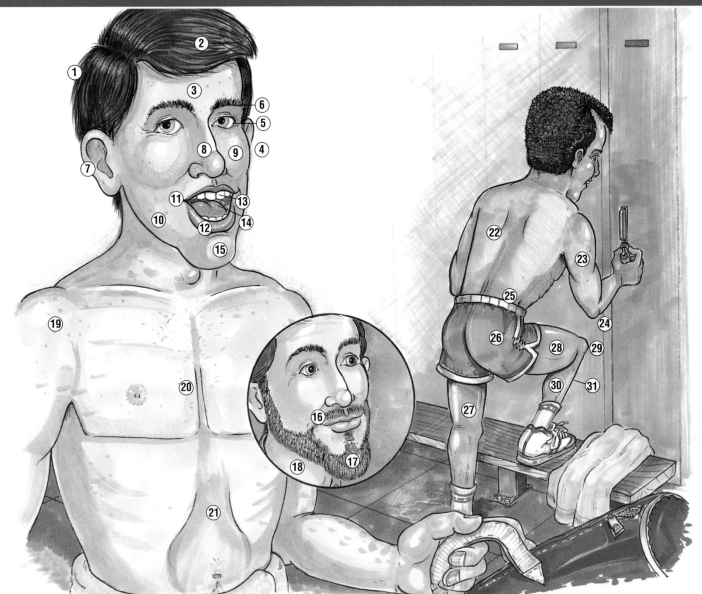

1. head
2. hair
3. forehead
4. face
5. eye
6. eyebrow
7. ear
8. nose
9. cheek
10. jaw
11. mouth
12. lip
13. tooth-teeth
14. tongue
15. chin
16. mustache
17. beard
18. neck
19. shoulder
20. chest
21. abdomen
22. back
23. arm
24. elbow
25. waist
26. hip
27. leg
28. thigh
29. knee
30. calf
31. shin

[1–15, 18–31]
A. My doctor checked my **head** and said everything is okay.
B. I'm glad to hear that.

Describe yourself as completely as you can.

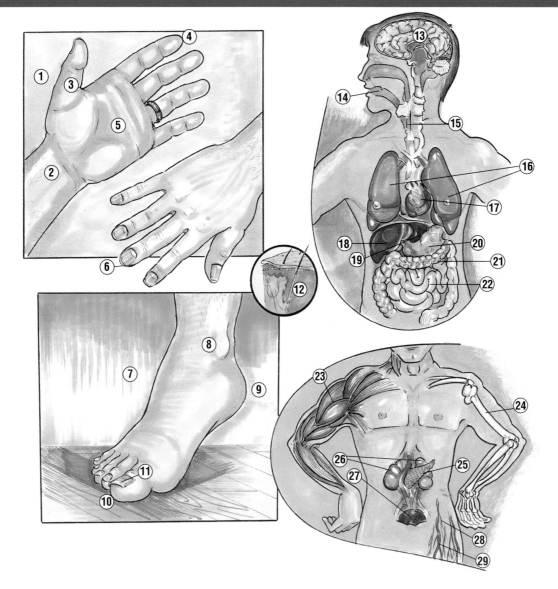

1. hand
2. wrist
3. thumb
4. finger
5. palm
6. fingernail
7. foot
8. ankle
9. heel
10. toe

11. toenail
12. skin
13. brain
14. throat
15. spinal cord
16. lungs
17. heart
18. liver
19. gallbladder
20. stomach

21. large intestine
22. small intestine
23. muscles
24. bones
25. pancreas
26. kidneys
27. bladder
28. veins
29. arteries

[1–11]
A. What's the matter?
B. I hurt my **hand**.

[12–29]
A. How am I, Doctor?
B. Well, I'm a little concerned about your **lungs**.

Which parts of the body on pages 114–117 are most important in school? at work? when you play your favorite sport?

1. headache
2. earache
3. toothache
4. stomachache
5. backache
6. sore throat
7. fever
8. cold
9. cough
10. virus
11. infection

12. rash
13. insect bite
14. sunburn
15. stiff neck
16. runny nose
17. bloody nose
18. cavity
19. wart
20. the hiccups
21. the chills

Tell about a time you had one of these problems.

A. What's the matter?
B. I have a/an ___[1–19]___ .

A. What's the matter?
B. I have ___[20–21]___ .

1. faint
2. dizzy
3. nauseous
4. bloated
5. congested
6. exhausted
7. cough
8. sneeze
9. wheeze
10. burp
11. vomit/throw up
12. bleed

13. twist
14. sprain
15. dislocate
16. scratch
17. scrape
18. bruise
19. burn
20. break–broke
21. hurt–hurt
22. cut–cut
23. swollen
24. itchy

A. What's the matter?
B. { I feel __[1–4]__ .
    I'm __[5–6]__ .
    I'm __[7–12]__ ing.

A. What's the matter?
B. { I __[13–22]__ ed my . . . .
    My . . . . is/are __[23–24]__ .

Tell about the last time you didn't feel well. What was the matter?

Tell about a time you hurt yourself. What happened?

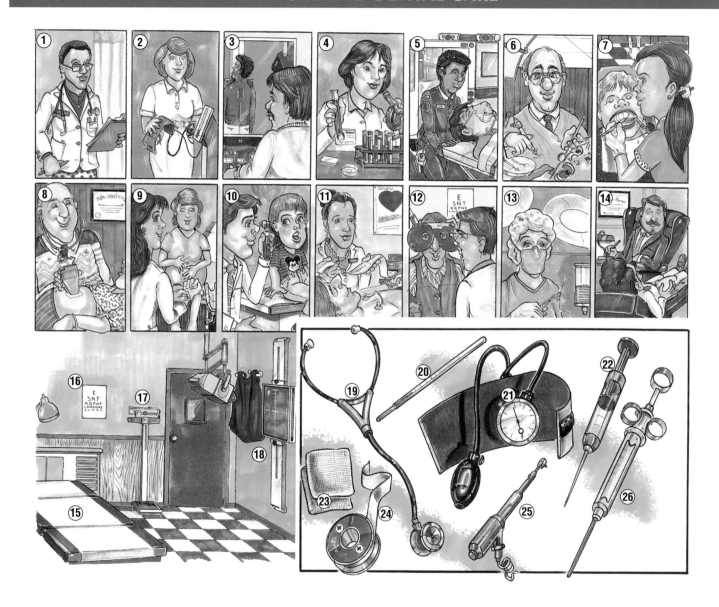

1. doctor
2. nurse
3. X-ray technician
4. lab technician
5. EMT/emergency medical technician
6. dentist
7. hygienist
8. obstetrician
9. gynecologist
10. pediatrician
11. cardiologist
12. optometrist
13. surgeon
14. psychiatrist
15. examination table
16. eye chart
17. scale
18. X-ray machine
19. stethoscope
20. thermometer
21. blood pressure gauge
22. needle
23. bandages
24. adhesive tape
25. drill
26. Novocaine

A. What do you do?
B. I'm a/an ___[1–14]___ .

A. Please step over here to the ___[15–18]___ .
B. Okay.

A. Please hand me the ___[19–26]___ .
B. Here you are.

Where do you go for medical care? How often?
Who examines you? What does he/she do?

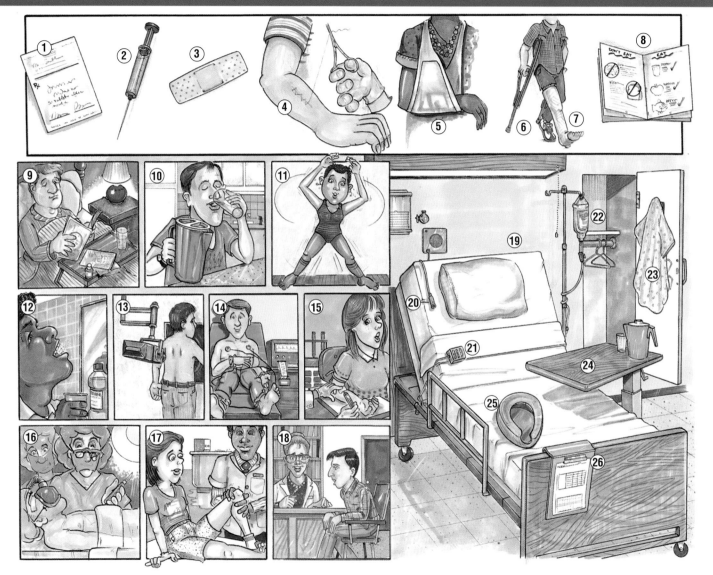

1. prescription
2. injection
3. bandaid
4. stitches
5. sling
6. crutches
7. cast
8. diet
9. rest in bed

10. drink fluids
11. exercise
12. gargle
13. X-rays
14. tests
15. blood tests
16. surgery
17. physical therapy
18. counseling

19. hospital bed
20. call button
21. bed control
22. I.V.
23. hospital gown
24. bed table
25. bed pan
26. medical chart

A. What did the doctor do?
B. She/He gave me (a/an) __[1–8]__.

A. What did the doctor say?
B. { I need to __[9–12]__.
   { I need __[13–18]__.

A. This is your __[19–26]__.
B. I see.

When did you have your last medical checkup?
What did the doctor say?

Tell about a time you were in the hospital.

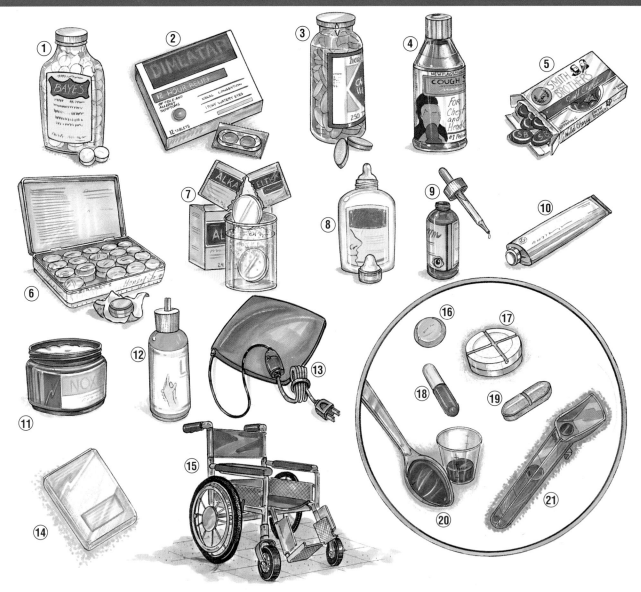

1. aspirin
2. cold tablets
3. vitamins
4. cough syrup
5. cough drops
6. throat lozenges
7. antacid tablets

8. decongestant spray/nasal spray
9. eye drops
10. ointment
11. creme
12. lotion
13. heating pad
14. ice pack

15. wheelchair
16. pill
17. tablet
18. capsule
19. caplet
20. teaspoon
21. tablespoon

A. What did the doctor say?
B. { I need to take __[1–4]__ .
    { I need to use (a/an) __[5–15]__ .

A. What's the dosage?
B. One __[16–21]__ , every three hours.

What medicines do you take or use?
For what ailments?

Describe any medical treatments or medicines in your country that are different from the ones in these lessons.

1. letter
2. postcard
3. aerogramme
4. package
5. first class
6. air mail
7. parcel post
8. book rate
9. registered mail
10. express mail

11. stamp
12. sheet of stamps
13. roll of stamps
14. book of stamps
15. money order
16. change-of-address form
17. selective service registration form
18. envelope
19. address

20. zip code
21. return address
22. stamp
23. window
24. postal worker/ postal clerk
25. stamp machine
26. mail truck
27. mailbox
28. letter carrier

A. Where are you going?
B. To the post office. I have to mail a/an __[1–4]__ .

A. How do you want to send it?
B. __[5–10]__ , please.

A. Next!
B. I'd like a __[11–17]__ , please.
A. Here you are.

A. I'll mail this letter for you.
B. Thanks.
A. Oops! You forgot the __[19–22]__ !

Describe the post office you use: How many windows are there? Is there a stamp machine? Are the postal workers friendly?

Tell about the postal system in your country.

1. librarian
2. checkout desk
3. library assistant
4. card catalog
5. shelves
6. information desk
7. atlas

8. encyclopedia
9. dictionary
10. newspaper
11. magazine
12. call card
13. library card

[1–11]
A. Excuse me. Where's/Where are the _____?
B. Over there.

Tell about the library you go to. Describe how to use the library.

1. office
2. nurse's office
3. guidance office
4. cafeteria
5. principal's office
6. classroom
7. locker
8. language lab
9. chemistry lab
10. teachers' lounge
11. gym
12. locker room

13. auditorium
14. field
15. bleachers
16. track
17. principal
18. assistant principal
19. school nurse
20. guidance counselor
21. driver's ed instructor
22. teacher
23. coach
24. custodian

A. Where are you going?
B. I'm going to the ___[1–16]___.*
A. Do you have a hall pass?
B. Yes. Here it is.

*With 6 and 7, use: I'm going to my _____.

A. Who's that?
B. That's the new ___[17–24]___.

Describe the school where you study English. Tell about the rooms, offices, and people.

Tell about differences between schools in the United States and in your country.

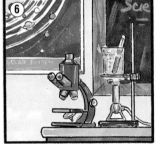

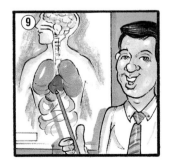

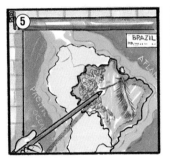

1. math
2. algebra
3. English
4. history
5. geography
6. science

7. Spanish
8. home economics
9. health
10. driver's ed
11. art
12. music

A. What do you have next period?
B. _____. How about you?
A. _____.

What is/was your favorite subject in school? Why?

1. band
2. orchestra
3. choir
4. drama
5. football

6. school newspaper
7. yearbook
8. literary magazine
9. student government

A. Are you going home right after school?
B. { No. I have __[1–5]__ practice.
   { No. I have a __[6–9]__ meeting.

What extracurricular activities do/did you participate in?

1. accountant
2. actor
3. actress
4. artist
5. assembler
6. barber

7. bricklayer
8. bus driver
9. butcher
10. carpenter
11. cashier

A. What do you do?
B. I'm an **accountant**.

Which of these occupations do you think is the most interesting? Why?

1. chef/cook
2. computer programmer
3. construction worker
4. custodian/janitor
5. delivery person
6. electrician
7. farmer
8. fisherman
9. foreman
10. gardener
11. hairdresser
12. housekeeper

A. What do you do?
B. I'm a **chef**.

Which of these occupations do you think is the most difficult? Why?

1. lawyer
2. mechanic
3. messenger
4. painter
5. pharmacist
6. plumber

7. police officer
8. repairperson
9. reporter
10. salesperson
11. sanitation worker

A. What's your occupation?
B. I'm a **lawyer**.
A. A **lawyer**?
B. Yes. That's right.

Which of these occupations do you think is the most important? Why?

1. scientist
2. seamstress
3. secretary
4. security guard
5. stock clerk
6. taxi driver

7. truck driver
8. veterinarian
9. waiter
10. waitress
11. welder

A. What do you do?
B. I'm a **scientist**. How about you?
A. I'm a **security guard**.

Do you work? What's your occupation? What are the occupations of the people in your family?

1. act
2. assemble *components*
3. build *things/*
   construct *things*
4. clean
5. cook
6. deliver *pizzas*

7. drive *a truck*
8. file
9. grow *vegetables*
10. guard *buildings*
11. mow *lawns*

A. Can you **act**?
B. Yes, I can.

Can you do any of these work activities? Which ones?

1. operate *equipment*
2. paint
3. play the *piano*
4. repair *things*/fix *things*
5. sell *cars*
6. serve *food*

7. sew
8. sing
9. teach
10. type
11. wash *dishes*
12. write

A. Do you know how to **operate** *equipment*?
B. Yes, I do.

Tell about your work abilities. What can you do?

1. time clock
2. time cards
3. supply room
4. safety glasses
5. masks
6. (assembly) line
7. worker
8. work station
9. foreman
10. machine
11. lever
12. fire extinguisher
13. first-aid kit
14. conveyor belt
15. warehouse
16. forklift
17. freight elevator
18. vending machine
19. suggestion box
20. cafeteria
21. shipping department
22. hand truck
23. loading dock
24. payroll office
25. personnel office

A. Excuse me. I'm a new employee.
   Where's/Where are the _____?
B. Next to/Near/In/On the _____.

A. Where's Fred?
B. He's in/on/at/next to/near
   the _____.

Are there any factories where you live?
What kind? What are the working conditions?

What products do factories in your country
produce?

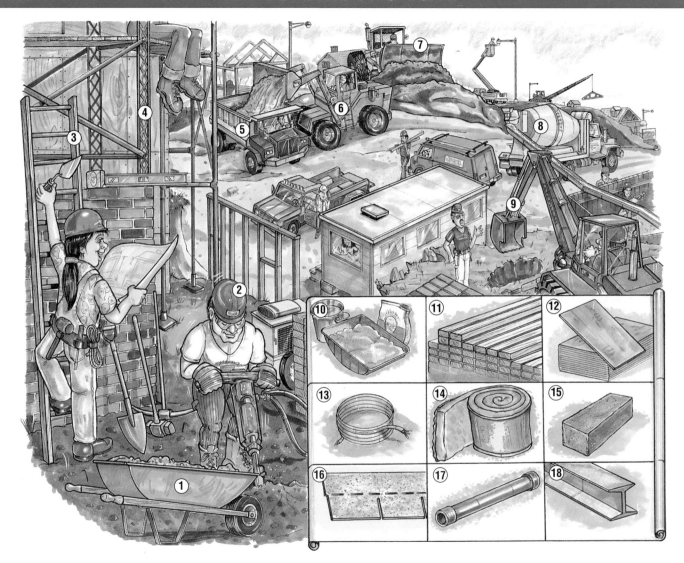

1. wheelbarrow
2. helmet
3. ladder
4. scaffolding
5. dump truck
6. front-end loader

7. bulldozer
8. cement mixer
9. backhoe
10. cement
11. wood/lumber
12. plywood

13. wire
14. insulation
15. brick
16. shingle
17. pipe
18. girder/beam

A. Could you get me that/those __[1-3]__?
B. Sure.

A. Watch out for that __[4-9]__!
B. Oh! Thanks for the warning!

A. Are we going to have enough __[10-14]/[15-18]__ s to finish the job?
B. I think so.

What building materials is your home made of?
Describe a construction site near your home or school.

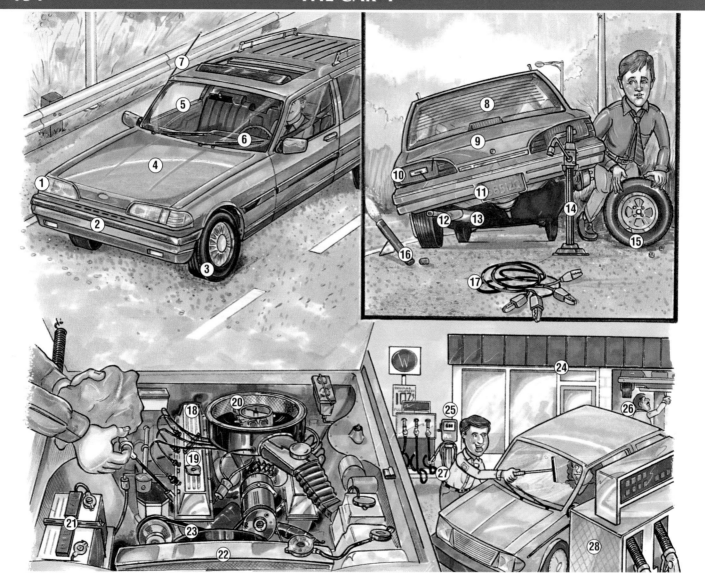

1. headlight
2. bumper
3. tire
4. hood
5. windshield
6. windshield wipers
7. antenna
8. rear defroster
9. trunk
10. taillight
11. license plate
12. tailpipe
13. muffler
14. jack
15. spare tire
16. flare
17. jumper cables
18. engine
19. spark plugs
20. carburetor
21. battery
22. radiator
23. fan belt
24. service station/ gas station
25. air pump
26. mechanic
27. attendant
28. gas pump

[1, 2, 4–8, 12, 13, 22, 23]
A. What's the matter with your car?
B. The _____(s) is/are broken.

[1, 3, 6, 7, 10, 19–21, 23]
A. Can I help you?
B. Yes. I need to replace a/the _____(s).

Do you own a car? Describe it.

1. visor
2. rearview mirror
3. dashboard
4. speedometer
5. turn signal
6. steering column
7. air bag
8. horn
9. ignition
10. radio
11. glove compartment
12. emergency brake
13. brake
14. accelerator/gas pedal
15. gearshift
16. automatic transmission
17. clutch
18. stickshift
19. manual transmission
20. shoulder harness
21. seat belt

A. The car has a very nice **visor**.
B. I see.

Describe the interior of a car you are familiar with.

A. train
1. train station
2. ticket window
3. schedule/timetable
4. train
5. track
6. passenger
7. conductor
8. luggage/baggage
9. porter
10. engine
11. engineer
12. passenger car
13. sleeper
14. dining car

B. bus
15. bus
16. bus driver
17. bus station
18. ticket counter

C. local bus
19. bus stop
20. rider/passenger

D. subway
21. subway station
22. subway
23. token booth
24. turnstile
25. token
26. fare card
27. fare card machine

E. taxi
28. taxi stand
29. taxi/cab
30. meter
31. cab driver/taxi driver

[A–E]
A. How are you going to get there?

B. { I'm going to take the __[A–D]__ .
{ I'm going to take a __[E]__ .

[1–5, 7–19, 21–24, 27, 28]
A. Excuse me. Where's the
   _____?
B. Over there.

How do you get to school or work? Describe public transportation where you live.

In your country, can you travel far by train or by bus? Where can you go? Describe the buses and trains.

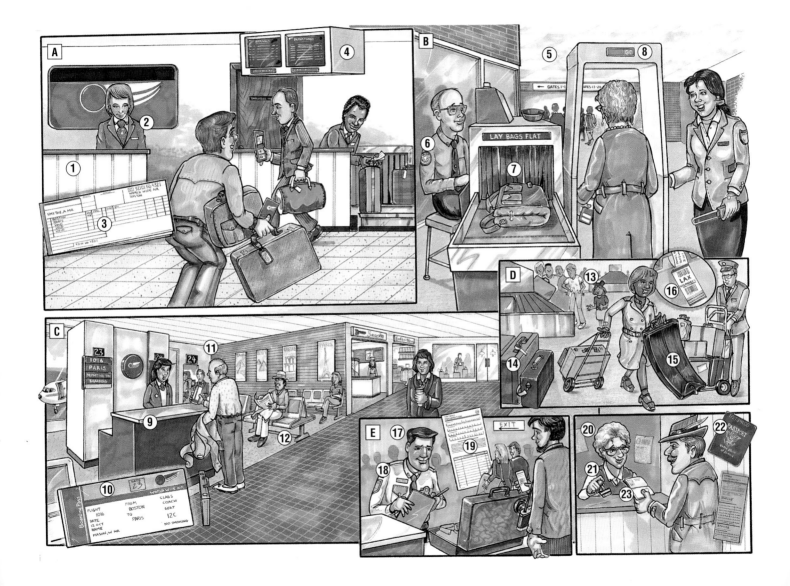

A. Check-In
1. ticket counter
2. ticket agent
3. ticket
4. arrival and departure monitor

B. Security
5. security checkpoint
6. security guard
7. X-ray machine
8. metal detector

C. The Gate
9. check-in counter
10. boarding pass
11. gate
12. waiting area

D. Baggage Claim
13. baggage claim area
14. suitcase
15. garment bag
16. baggage claim check

E. Customs and Immigration
17. customs
18. customs officer
19. customs declaration form
20. immigration
21. immigration officer
22. passport
23. visa

[1, 2, 4–9, 11–13, 17, 18, 20, 21]
A. Excuse me. Where's the _____?*
B. Right over there.

*With 17 and 20, use: Excuse me. Where's _____?

[3, 10, 14–16, 19, 22, 23]
A. Oh, no! I lost my _____!
B. I'll help you look for it.

Describe an airport you are familiar with.
Tell about a time you went through Customs and Immigration.

A. Weather

1. sunny
2. cloudy
3. clear
4. hazy
5. foggy
6. windy
7. humid/muggy
8. raining
9. drizzling
10. snowing
11. hailing
12. sleeting
13. lightning
14. thunderstorm
15. snowstorm
16. hurricane/typhoon
17. tornado

B. Temperature

18. thermometer
19. Fahrenheit
20. Centigrade/Celsius

21. hot
22. warm
23. cool
24. cold
25. freezing

C. Seasons

26. summer
27. fall/autumn
28. winter
29. spring

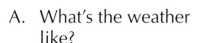

A. What's the weather like?
B. It's [1–12] .

A. What's the weather forecast?
B. There's going to be [13] /a [14–17] .

A. How's the weather?
B. It's [21–25] .
A. What's the temperature?
B. It's . . . . degrees [19,20] .

Describe the seasons where you live.
Tell about the weather and the temperature.

What's your favorite season?
Why?

1. jogging
2. running
3. walking
4. roller skating
5. bicycling
6. skiing
7. skating
8. sailing

9. swimming
10. fishing
11. tennis
12. baseball
13. football
14. basketball
15. soccer

A. What do you like to do in your free time?

B. { I like to go   [1–10] .
     I like to play   [11–15] .

Do you do any of these activities? Which ones? Which are popular in your country?

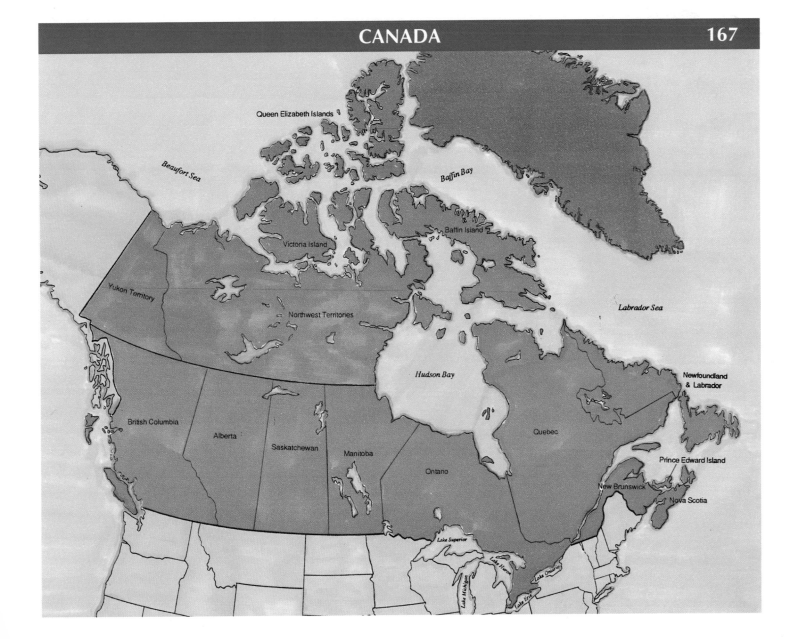

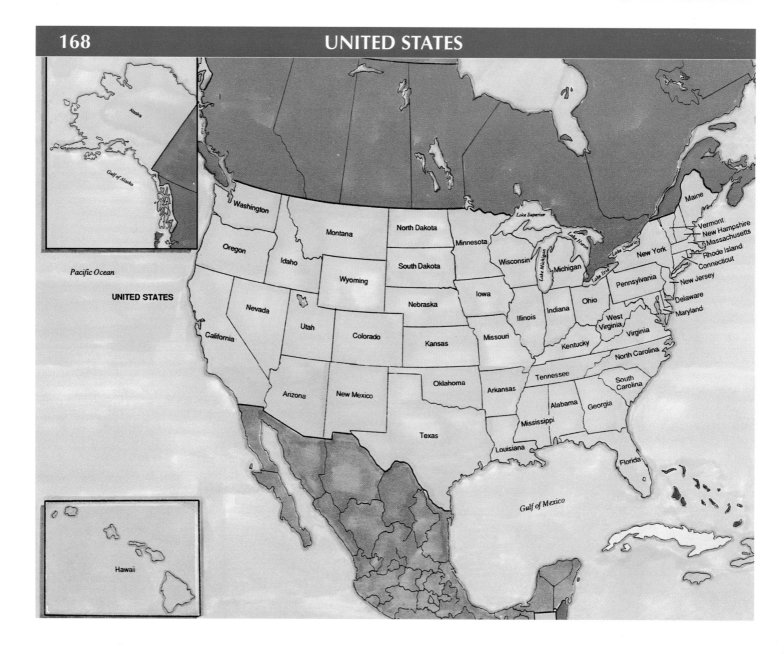

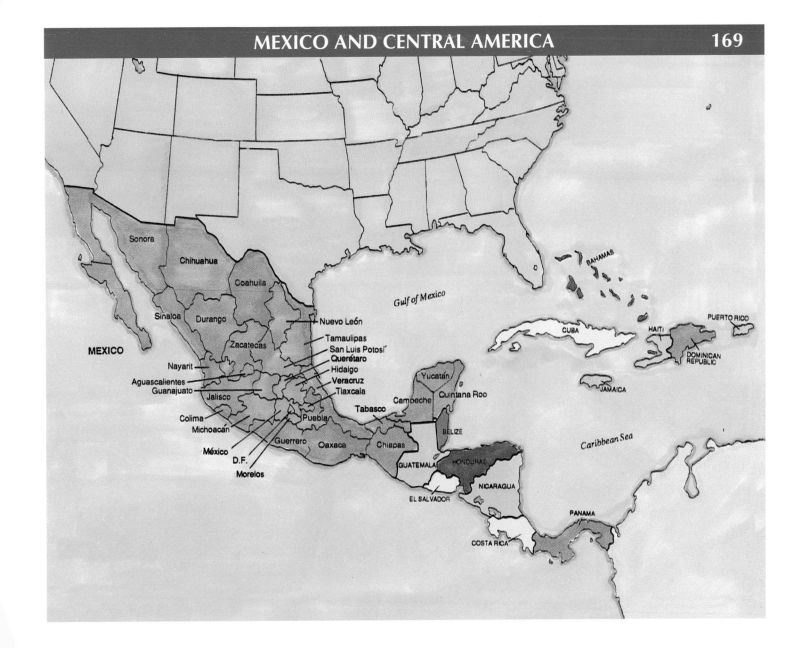

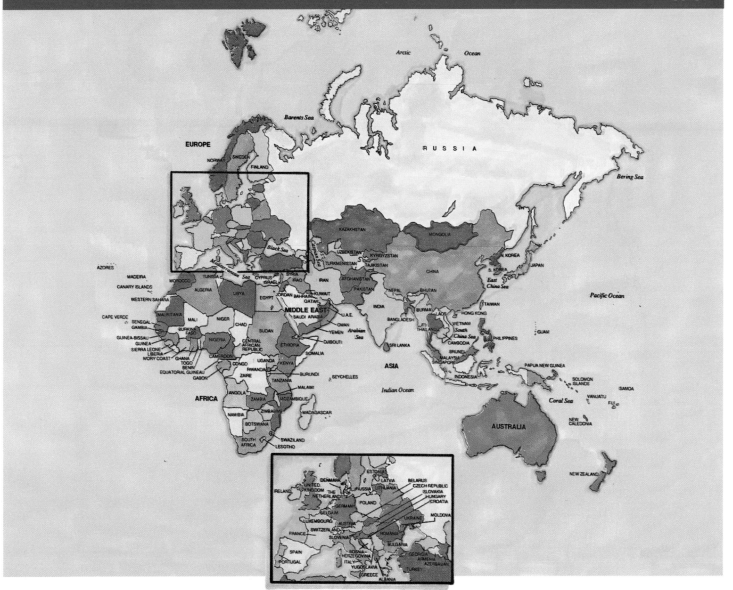

teaspoon	tablespoon	1 (fluid) ounce	cup
tsp.	Tbsp.	1 fl. oz.	8 fl. ozs.

pint	quart	gallon
pt.	qt.	gal.
16 fl. ozs.	32 fl. ozs.	128 fl. ozs.

an ounce	a quarter of a pound	half a pound	three-quarters of a pound	a pound
oz.	¼ lb.	½ lb.	¾ lb.	lb.
	4 ozs.	8 ozs.	12 ozs.	16 ozs.

The bold number indicates the page(s) on which the word appears; the number that follows indicates the word's location in the illustration and in the word list on the page. For example, "apple 77-1" indicates that the word *apple* is on page 77 and is item number 1.

THEMATIC INDEX